AF421493

PERCY
The Angry Fire Engine

A story by Clara Lim
Illustration by Octaviani Isabella

For ages 2-5

tots PUBLISHING
content transcends technology

This is Percy.
"Hello!" Percy says.

1

Percy is a fire engine that
drives firemen to put out fires.

Percy likes to show off his shiny coat of red paint to the people of Sunnydale.

Percy is very excited because fireman Steve is going to drive him in the Sunnydale annual parade.

Percy is on his lunch break with the other engines when Harold comes racing up to him.

"Hello Percy! Guess what? Fireman
Steve has decided to drive me in
the Sunnydale parade!"

"What?" Percy exclaims. "He promised me I would be in the parade!"

"Fireman Steve says you're too big of an engine and you can't fit under the bridge."

8

Percy turns very red and feels angry. He is jealous that Harold has taken his place.

"How could you take my place?"
Percy bellows at Harold.

He is so angry that he drives headfirst into a fire extinguisher and breaks it!

The fire extinguisher explodes.
Chemicals rain all over the engines!

Some of the engines are so horrified that they drive off and seek shelter in another building.

Sam and Carla are furious with Percy.

"You need to control your temper, Percy!" Sam snaps.

"You have ruined our paint!" Carla adds.

Percy is not sorry and continues
with his tantrum. He shouts
nasty things at Harold.

"You're a selfish little engine,
Harold! You're so small that no one
will even see you in the parade!"

Finally Harold decides he must fetch fireman Steve to settle the problem.

19

When the engines return to the fire station they ignore Percy completely.

Fireman Steve hears about the incident and comes to the fire station to investigate.

"Percy, you have been a very naughty fire engine," he says. "How could you lose your temper?" Steve demands to know.

"I am angry that Harold is going to be in the parade, and I'm not!" Percy cries.

"That is no excuse to behave
badly. Everyone has to accept
things they don't like sometimes."

Percy is sad that everyone is angry with him and ignoring him. He decides to apologize.

"I'm sorry that I lost my temper, everyone, and I'm very sorry I shouted at you Harold," he says remorsefully.

"That's alright," Harold says.
"We can be friends again."

Now Percy goes to a quiet place to calm down whenever he gets angry.

Since fireman Steve is so pleased with Percy's changed behavior he promises to bring Percy along for the first part of the parade!

tots PUBLISHING
content transcends technology

Other stories in this series:

Fun educational applications

Phonics Train

Speed Flashcard

Letter Race

Animal Matching

Every child deserves the best education.

Enhancing children's development, making learning fun! Tots Publishing helps to spark young ones to think, do and express themselves as they learn.

See the full list of applications at totsapps.com

ISBN 978-981-08-9695-9